THE LITTLE
BOOK OF

WIT & WISDOM

GW00670024

Dalesman

First published in Great Britain 2003 by
Dalesman Publishing
The Water Mill, Broughton Hall
Skipton, North Yorkshire BD23 3AG

Reprinted 2004

A British Library Cataloguing-in-Publication record
is available for this book

ISBN 1 85568 209 5

Origination by Grasmere Digital Imaging Limited
Printed by Amadeus Press, Cleckheaton, West Yorkshire

Also in this series:

THE LITTLE BOOK OF YORKSHIRE
ISBN 1 85568 194 3

THE LITTLE BOOK OF THE LAKE DISTRICT
ISBN 1 85568 200 1

INTRODUCTION

Since 1953, Old Amos has been a regular and much-loved feature of *Dalesman* magazine. His creator Rowland Lindup first submitted some cartoons to the *Dalesman* editor Harry J Scott, who liked what he saw and asked Rowland to submit further ideas.

'The first Old Amos drawing wasn't a bit like those I draw of him today,' recalled Rowland in 1988. 'However, Harry Scott was so taken by the idea of a monthly character with a witty saying that he invited me to let him have a series. The name Old Amos comes from an old gentleman who lived near us years ago.

'Once I discovered Amos was going to be a regular feature in *Dalesman*, I had to improve on the original drawings. Gradually I got him as I liked to see him.'

Rowland Lindup spent most of his life in Leeds, and then made his home in Blackpool until his death in 1989. Since then, Old Amos has been drawn by Rowland's son Pete.

So enjoy this 'little' selection from fifty years of humour and wisdom from the old chap who doesn't look a day older than when he first appeared in the magazine.

It takes less time to do summat useful than it does to explain why tha didn't.

It's sometimes best to look for new worries than brood over t' owd uns.

Ah reckon moderation is all right as long as tha don't overdo it.

**Why give up bad habits when tha feels
no better for it?**

**Tha knows tha's gettin' old when
tha has to take a rest afore
takin' a nap.**

Has tha noticed how folk thi own age are allus older than thissen?

Ah reckon a man's weakness is sometimes t' strongest thing abaht him.

A man's mind is like a shop
— no good if it's allus closed.

Why does it take so long to find summat tha's lost when losing it took no time at all?

Ah reckon it's best to make future plans — otherwise tha wouldn't have owt to cancel.

It's Christmas, a time when
t' past should be forgotten ...
but t' present remembered.

**How can 'appiness and joy be inspired
by a little fat old bloke with a long
white beard?**

Ah reckon a man's mind can be just like cement — all mixed up and permanently set.

**Ah reckon fellas can only agree on
things that don't interest 'em.**

Ah've allus enjoyed a long walk, especially if it's taken by someone who annoys me.

By 'eck — if Ah 'ad to spend that much, Ah wouldn't be able to sleep at night.

Strange how dull minds and sharp tongues allus go together.

**Ah reckon folk would get on better
if they raised their hats instead
of their voices.**

There's summat up wi' this un — all Ah can 'ear is an engaged signal.

**Being an owd fool isn't easy
— tha 'as to work at it.**

If tha hasn't many faults, make sure tha makes t' best on 'em.

**Don't fret over a small crisis —
there's bound to be a bigger un
to worry abaht.**

Education is what tha 'as when tha's forgotten what tha's learnt.

When Ah were young, Ah thought Ah knew all t' answers — now Ah don't even understand t' questions.

Ah've a place for everything in
my 'ouse. T' trouble is, Ah usually
put it somewhere else.

A good memory is a useful thing for forgettin' things wi'.

**Ah reckon a man starts behavin'
'imself when there's nowt
else 'e can do.**

**Us owd fowk like to give good advice
'cos we're no longer able to set
bad examples.**

Ah well, it's probably better to waste
time than do nowt wi' it.

It's no use shoppin' for new ideas in a mind that's closed.

**Tha 'as to believe in luck, or 'ow else
could fowk tha doesn't like become
successful.**

'A fool and 'is money are soon parted'
— makes tha wonder 'ow they got
together in t' first place.

'As tha thowt of marriage as an investment? It pays thee dividends, if tha pays interest.

**Ah reckon it's a rum world: tha can't
live because o' income tax, and tha
daren't die for fear o' death duties.**

**Ah've lived 'alf me life in t' village
— now Ah can't wait to start
t' second 'alf.**

**Ah reckon that knowin' what tha says
is better than sayin' what tha knows.**

This 'ud be a much better world if folk
thought more abaht brass bands an'
less abaht brass.

Ah wish they would sing these 'ere operas in English — then Ah could understand what were borin' me.

**A real friend is somebody who knows
all abaht thi, and despite that is still
thi friend.**

**A good disposition is like a bus pass
— tha can't get on without it.**

**Makin' both ends meet doesn't allus
mean that they'll like each other.**

T' best labour-savin' device we have today is — tomorrow.

Ah reckon more fowk are knocked down by a fast tongue than a fast car.

**Tongue waggin' is t' most exercise
some fowk get.**

If tha gets carried away wi' thi own importance, tha won't 'ave far to walk back.

**A chap may be a poor 'usband,
but he was once a rich bachelor.**

**Try not to be too downhearted 'cos
t' years are passin' by — be grateful
that they keep turnin' up.**

Is tha like me? Get up in t' mornin'
wi' nowt to do — and at bedtime
there's still 'alf on it undone?

**If tha can be alone wi' thi thoughts,
tha's in good company.**

To make a fool of 'imself, a man needs only one thing — opportunity.

**Surprisin' how many fowks suffer
from an interferiority complex.**

Fowk 'at think t' least, talk t' most.

Who said that trees were t' best efficiency experts? Ah think nowt o' their loose-leaf system.

Ah reckon this is t' season when all
t' cock birds feel gallant and all
t' lady birds feel buoyant.

She's just told me that dark-headed men marry first, but Ah thowt it were t' light-headed ones.

We suffer more from troubles
'at nivver come than from all
t' misfortunes we 'ave to face.

**When we go to t' library, it's like
turnin' sheep into a field — we all
find our own pasture best.**

**If tha's startin' a library, t' first book
should be a bank book.**

Ah reckon when a chap admits he was wrong yesterday, he's wiser today.

A wise man's ignorant o' things that are not worth knowin'.

Ah reckon that 'liking' comes an' goes.
Love lasts.

Ah reckon t' forward lasses cast many
a backward glance.

T' best time to start a task is when tha's not in t' mood — tha'll make a better job on it.

T' big advantage of 'avin' nowt to do is that tha can start whenever tha wants.

Yon rent man is t' most popular chap
in t' village. Fowk are allus askin'
'im to call again.

**Tha knows what an 'ousing estate is?
That's where they cut all t' trees
down an' name t' streets after 'em.**

'Ave yer noticed 'ow some fowk are
like blisters — they only appear when
all t' work's done?

**First rule o' successful gardenin'
— plant thissen in a comfy chair.**

Lots o' fowk use sign language these days — they sign for everything.

**Ah bet if we all 'ad a magic lamp,
there'd be a tax on genies.**

**Intelligence is like this 'ere stream
— when it's deepest it makes
less noise.**

**Keep cheerful — a smile nivver goes
up in price or down in value.**

This 'ere is one o' them chaps who
runs out o' conversation afore
they run out o' words.

Some fellahs can give up smokin' and drinkin' — but they can't give up talkin' abaht it.

These days Ah reckon there's no such thing as an idle rumour — they're all busy.

In our village, a fellah is known by 'is first name — an' 'is last scandal.

Ah reckon if a chap can't be a star,
he needn't be a cloud.

Ah reckon second thoughts are t' best — but they're nearly allus too late.

**Tha must make t' most of thissen;
it's all tha's gettin'.**

**Ah reckon there's more to life than
tryin' to make it go quicker.**

Ah reckon t' best place for a picnic is allus a little farther on.

T' trouble is havin' a place for everything is 'ow it gets filled up wi' everything else.

**Middle age is when tha starts eatin'
what's good for you instead of
what tha likes.**

Ah reckon t' best way of answerin' a bad argument is to let it go on.

It doesn't matter what tha does,
there's allus somebody who knew
tha would.

A naughty boy's like a spot — keep
pickin' at 'im, and 'e'll never get better.

**Some people's idea of keepin' a secret
is to whisper it.**

Some fowk 'ud think they were only
'alf-dressed unless they 'ad a chip
on t' shoulder.

Real problem wi' leisure time is stoppin' other fowk usin' yours.

Some fowk sit in t' fields watchin' cars go by. Other fowk sit in cars watchin' fields go by.

**She's a woman of few words — but she
uses 'em an 'eck of a lot.**

**Yon chap's 'ad so much 'elp in life,
'e's 'elpless.**

T' 'ardest work of all is doin' nowt.

**For some fowk, retirement's taken
all t' fun out o' Saturdays.**

**Shop bacon's cut so thin these days,
tha can taste t' knife.**

**Ah reckon t' chap wi' nowt to boast
of except his ancestors is like a
potato — t' best part's underground.**

It's odd that fowk who 'ave statues are usually forgotten. Them as do things tha remembers 'ave no statues.

**When bairns are quiet, it doesn't allus
mean they're plannin' mischief.
They may 'ave done it already.**

Spring allus reminds me that worry is like a rocking-horse — it keeps movin' but gets thi nowhere.

**The only difference between April and
March is that tha expects it in March.**

Ah reckon 'horse sense' is what keeps a horse from bettin' on a man.

**Ah reckon money doesn't go very far
these days but, by gow, it stays away
a long time.**

Ah remember when fowk were amazed when chaps in cars drove at 15 miles an hour — and they still are.

When a man says he doesn't know
which way to turn for t' best, he's
probably drivin'.

Ah reckon that worry is a good thing after all, for t' thing tha worries abaht nivver 'appens.

Maybe it's better to fettle an' shout abaht it, than nivver to fettle at all.

**Ah allus says that dignity is t' one
thing tha can't preserve in a'cohol.**

Ah were asked to look after mi grandson, but Ah told 'em Ah believe in sparin' t' child and usin' t' rod.

It seems to me 'at ivvery man in this world reaps what he sows, except t' poor gardener.

Yon chap can trace 'is family tree all t' way back to t' days when 'is family lived in it.

**Ah reckon we should do like yon owl
— think twice afore we speak or,
better still, just keep on thinkin'.**

Some fowk can stay longer in an hour than others can in a week.

**Yon chap does t' 'ardest work of t' day
before breakfast — gettin' up.**

**Too many fowk think they can push
'emselves forward by givvin'
'emselves a pat on t' back.**

**Poverty wouldn't be 'alf as bad to bide
if other fowk didn't know it.**

**It's easier to find a fault
than to lose one.**

With this 'ere Health Service, a doctor a day is cheaper than apples, Ah reckon.

Ah reckon a man's as young as 'e feels — but never as impressive to small boys.

Ah've 'eard that t' town hall can be evacuated in two minutes. Ah bet our village quartet could do it in less.

**Ah reckon that 'women's intuition'
is that what tells 'er she's right
— whether she is or not.**

This is what tha might call 'risin' wi' t' lark'.

**A gardener's nobbut another name
for an ornithologist; he spends 'is
day feedin' wild birds.**

For a full list of books, calendars,
videos, cassettes and magazines visit
www.dalesman.co.uk